Facts About the California Sea Lion

By Lisa Strattin

© 2016 Lisa Strattin

Revised 2022 © Lisa Strattin

FREE BOOK

FREE FOR ALL SUBSCRIBERS

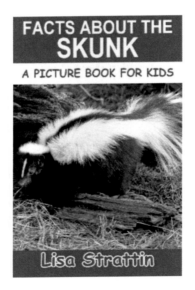

LisaStrattin.com/Subscribe-Here

BOX SET

- **FACTS ABOUT THE POISON DART FROGS**
- **FACTS ABOUT THE THREE TOED SLOTH**
  - **FACTS ABOUT THE RED PANDA**
  - **FACTS ABOUT THE SEAHORSE**
  - **FACTS ABOUT THE PLATYPUS**
  - **FACTS ABOUT THE REINDEER**
  - **FACTS ABOUT THE PANTHER**
- **FACTS ABOUT THE SIBERIAN HUSKY**

LisaStrattin.com/BookBundle

Facts for Kids Picture Books by Lisa Strattin

Little Blue Penguin, Vol 92

Chipmunk, Vol 5

Frilled Lizard, Vol 39

Blue and Gold Macaw, Vol 13

Poison Dart Frogs, Vol 50

Blue Tarantula, Vol 115

African Elephants, Vol 8

Amur Leopard, Vol 89

Sabre Tooth Tiger, Vol 167

Baboon, Vol 174

Sign Up for New Release Emails Here

LisaStrattin.com/subscribe-here

Contents

INTRODUCTION

Known for their intelligence, playfulness and noisy barking, the California Sea Lions can be said to be well adapted to the semi-aquatic life style. They swim using their front flippers and are agile on land. They are also able to control their hind flippers independently. They are good swimmers and can float together on the ocean surface in "rafts."

APPEARANCE

California Sea Lions have a dog-like face and at a young age the males develop a bony bump on top of their skull. The color of the different sexes also varies, for a male it is chocolate brown compared to females who are a golden brown. A grown male can weigh up to 390 pounds and be seven feet in length; the female can grow up to 220 pounds and six feet in length.

LIFE STAGES

These mammals mostly breed on land during June and July. The males mark their territories and are often very aggressive to other males. They use calls and loud barks to encourage other females to join them. The females group themselves into harems for specific males. The size of each group depends on how strong the male is.

Females give birth to pups who weigh between 6 – 9 kg each. They nurse for about six months.

Age classes from birth to adulthood include:

1)   A pup where the age is less than one year.

2)   A yearling is 1-2 years old.

3)   A juvenile is 2-4 years old.

4)   A sub-adult – for males it is 4-8 years old and for females it is 2-5 years of age.

5)   An adult is when the male is 8 years old and the female is 5 years old.

HABITAT

The California Sea Lions live in several parts of the world, from Southeast Alaska to central Mexico, and also in the Gulf of California.

DIET

California Sea Lions are opportunistic feeders, this means they are not picky about what they consume because they like to eat a lot of food each day. Their main diet includes squids, octopus, herring, rockfish, mackerel, and small sharks.

FRIENDS AND ENEMIES

California Sea lions are very friendly to people.

The Great White Sharks prey on them, so these are their enemy.

SUITABILITY AS A PET

Due to their high intelligence and calm nature, California Sea Lions are easy to handle as pets by professionals. But because of their size and needs, they are not good as pets for kids.

They also help biologists and researchers in studying Sea Lion behavior. For the most part, the interactions they have with humans have been very good. They are also a popular choice for public display in zoos, and oceanariums.

They are quick learners and have been trained by the United States Navy for military operations.

COLOR ME

COLOR ME

COLOR ME

COLOR ME

COLOR ME

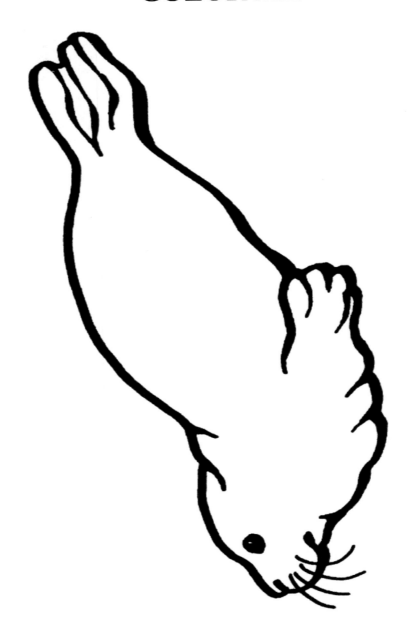

COLOR ME

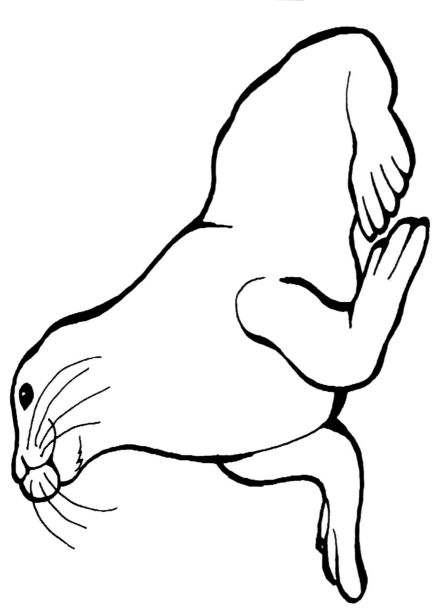

COLOR ME

COLOR ME

COLOR ME

COLOR ME

Please leave me a review here:

LisaStrattin.com/Review-Vol-19

For more Kindle Downloads Visit Lisa Strattin Author Page on Amazon Author Central

amazon.com/author/lisastrattin

To see upcoming titles, visit my website at LisaStrattin.com– most books available on Kindle!

LisaStrattin.com

FREE BOOK

FOR ALL SUBSCRIBERS – SIGN UP NOW

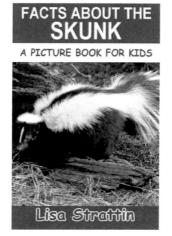

LisaStrattin.com/Subscribe-Here

LisaStrattin.com/Facebook

LisaStrattin.com/Youtube

Made in the USA
Middletown, DE
01 May 2023

29854078R00022